CW00435433

STATE OF THE CONTROVERSY

BETWIXT

UNITED AND SEPARATE PARLIAMENTS

ANDREW FLETCHER OF SALTOUN

with an Introduction by P. H. Scott

Printed for The Saltire Society by
WILLIAM BLACKWOOD
Edinburgh 1982

INTRODUCTION

As far as I can discover, this is the first time that this pamphlet has been reprinted since it was included as an Appendix to the two editions of Sir John Dalrymple's *Memoirs of Great Britain and Ireland* in 1788 and 1790. It originally appeared as a separate pamphlet in 1706, published anonymously as was the usual practice of the time. It was reprinted, rather imperfectly, in the same year. Since then, only the Dalrymple reprints have rescued it from oblivion. It was not included in the collected *Political Works* of Andrew Fletcher, of which the first edition was published in London in 1732, sixteen years after his death. It is also omitted from David Daiches's very useful *Selected Political Writings and Speeches of Andrew Fletcher of Saltoun*, published by the Scottish Academic Press in 1979.

The original pamphlet of 1706 is, of course, now very rare, but there are copies in the National Library of Scotland and the British Library. The present text follows the copy in the National Library.

Since the pamphlet was issued anonymously, and we had no record that Andrew Fletcher ever laid claim to it, we cannot be absolutely certain that he was the author. There are, however, strong grounds for believing that he did. When Dalrymple reprinted the text, he gave his reasons for the attribution to Fletcher in a passage which is worth quoting in full:

"The late Mr Fletcher of the House of Commons, once put into my hands, as related in common with him to Mr Fletcher of Salton, whose family he represented, a treatise on the Union of States, which he found among the papers of his ancestor, but not written with his hand, desiring my opinion whether it was his composition. I thought that it was. Afterwards I found a copy of this paper in the Advocates Library, and on it, in the hand-writing of Mr Thomas Rudiman librarian, who was the contemporary of Mr Fletcher, and eminent for historical erudition, industry and accuracy, the following note, 'supposed to be written by the Laird of Salton'. Mr Fletcher's style is easily known, because every word has a precise meaning, and distinct from any other in the sentence; the structure of the sentence is as simple, but as varied as that which is used in private conversation; the method in his composition is perfectly regular, but artfully concealed; and one singularity in his reasoning is, that the arguments are placed in an order to derive force from what went before, and to give force to what comes after, so as to seem to grow out of each other. But, above all, when he is animated with passion, his flashes are sometimes as quick as lightning, and sometimes followed by a thunder of period: All which mark an original genius, but made chaste by the reading of the ancients. The volume of his works is unequally collected, and his discourse on the affairs of Spain is a poor translation from the Italian, in which he wrote it."

R. A. Scott Macfie, who wrote a very detailed and scholarly *Bibliography of Andrew Fletcher of Saltoun* (Publications of the Edinburgh Bibliographical Society, Vol. IV, 1901), also accepts that the pamphlet is Fletcher's. "The style", he says, "is more jerky than was usual with Fletcher, but it may have been composed hurriedly. The ideas are in harmony with what he expressed elsewhere."

Dalrymple is not alone in finding Fletcher's prose style both admirable and distinctive. Francis Espinasse, in his article on Fletcher in *The Dictionary of National Biography* says: "As a writer he is superior to any Scotsman of his age, and his oratory, nervous and incisive, is made eloquent by his sincerity and earnestness." It is perhaps true, as Scott Macfie says elsewhere in his paper, having struggled to distinguish the real from the false among the works attributed to Fletcher: "These who are bold enough to attempt the task will find that the difficulty of identifying Fletcher's style is much under-rated by Dalrymple." This is a matter of personal judgement. My own feeling is that Fletcher's style is recognizable among Scots writers of the period not in the "thunder of period" in Dalrymple's words, but in the very different qualities which he also mentions of conversational simplicity and lighting strokes. Take, for instance, this sentence from the present pamphlet: "This will be the issue of that darling Plea, of being one and not two; it will be turned upon the Scots with a Vengeance; and their 45 Scots Members may dance round to all Eternity, in this Trap of their own making." This has an idiomatic ease and a verbal dexterity remarkable in a Scotsman of the period writing in a language

which no one in Scotland then spoke. Towards the end of the
18th Century such men as William Robertson, Adam Fergus-
son and David Hume, though still speaking Scots, had
laboriously evolved an effective, but rather Latinate and
ponderous, English prose in their writing. The English officer,
Edward Topham, who spent six months in Edinburgh between
1774 and 1775, said of them, "I shall only say, that they appear
to me, from their conversation, to write English as a foreign
tongue; their mode of talking, phrase and expression, but little
resembling the language of their works". Their style in writing
owed more to the influence of the Latin in which they were
steeped in school than to the rhythms of English speech which
they seldom heard. As Lord Mansfield said to Alexander
Carlyle, the histories of Hume and Robertson did not sound to
him as though they were in English.

How then is it that we find Fletcher, nearly a century before
Hume, writing English with such conversational familiarity
and confidence? As far as we know, he made only short visits to
England itself, including a disastrous and very brief partici-
pation in Monmouth's rebellion. Probably his main exposure
to English speech was the time he spent as a political refugee
in Holland in the circles of both Monmouth and William. He
presumably had a quick ear for language, as appears also from
the very creditable Italian in which he wrote one of his
pamphlets. We may well regret that a Scotsman, renowned for
his patriotism and addressing his own countrymen on a Scottish
question, should even before the Union have recourse to
English. The tradition had been established even by then,
under the influence of the Authorised Version of the Bible and
the practice of the Kirk, that English prose was the appropriate
language for written argument on serious issues. The fact at all
events is that Fletcher managed it with a dexterity well in
advance of his time. In many ways he anticipated the men of the
Enlightenment, in the boldness and originality of his thought,
and his concern for social questions and economic improvement. In his handling of English, he easily excelled them.

If Scott Macfie had some hesitation in attributing the
pamphlet to Fletcher on the internal evidence of style alone, he
seems to have no doubt that the arguments were entirely
consistent with Fletcher's other writings. Certainly, his voice is
unmistakable in his robust rejection of the incorporating
Union. "The Scots deserve no pity, if they voluntarily surrender

their united and separate interests to the Mercy of an united Parliament, where the English shall have so vast a Majority." At the same time, there are one or two apparent inconsistencies. Fletcher's approval of Union in another sense is not one of these, as in the second sentence of the pamphlet: "All well-meaning Men have thought, that a nearer Union will be the only effectual measure to bring these Two Nations to a peaceable State at home, and to make them formidable abroad." Throughout the whole controversy, Fletcher constantly argued for both national independence and international co-operation to preserve peace and promote trade. In this, as in other respects, his political thought is still remarkably apposite. In 1707 the word "Union" acquired a special meaning in this context, but its normal meaning before then had been the absence of discord or any form of association for any common purpose. It is in this sense that Fletcher uses the word. To him it meant an equitable association between free and autonomous states. (This point is discussed more fully in chapter 4 of my *1707: The Union of Scotland and England*; Chambers, 1979.)

The real inconsistencies with Fletcher's known attitude appear on pages 31 and 33: "I am not for over-loading the Power of the Prince with unusual Limitations, especially during the Administration of so gentle a Government as we live now under at present" and "but if a Scots Parliament does extert themselves according to their Duty, they have a Gracious Queen who will do them Justice". Fletcher was no enthusiast for monarchy. "Tell King William from me" he said to the Duke of Hamilton "that he has not as good a right to his crown as I have to my estate", and he once suggested that the idea of hereditary monarchy was as absurd as a hereditary professionship would be. Not surprisingly, some of his contemporaries and subsequent historians have described him as a republican. In fact, in his known speeches and writings, he never argued for the abolition of monarchy, but only for the transfer of effective power from the Crown to the Parliament. From 1703 to 1706, he struggled hard in the Parliament at Edinburgh precisely for "limitations"—his own words—on the right of the Monarch to intervene in Scottish affairs. Since James VI went to London in 1603, the Crown had retained wide executive powers, including the right to appoint state officials with all the patronage that went with it, and could withhold assent to Acts of the Scottish Parliament. These powers were exercised in the name of the Queen by the English ministers. This "perpetual enslaving of their nation to the ministers of England", as Fletcher called it in one of his speeches, had become intolerable in Scotland. Fletcher's "limitations", which were adopted in part by the Scottish Parliament, were designed to curb this Royal, or English ministerial, power.

How then do we account for this soft-pedalling of the idea of limitations and the flattering references to Queen Anne and her Government? They may, of course, be ironic. In any case, this pamphlet was addressed to a particular moment of crisis in the events which led to 1707. It is clear from its date and its content that it was written and printed, presumably in great haste, between the conclusion of the negotiation (if that is what it can be called) in Whitehall on 11 July 1706 and the opening of the debate in the Scottish Parliament on 3 October. The terms of the draft Treaty were not immediately published but gradually leaked out. Obviously, there was an urgent need to rally opposition while there was still time. The pamphlet has all the urgency and immediacy of a letter to the newspapers on a desperate and pressing issue. The "limitations" no longer mattered, in comparison to the threat to the very survival of the Scottish Parliament.

On the whole, therefore, I think that we may agree with the later Fletcher, Dalrymple, Rudiman and Scott Macfie that the present pamphlet is indeed by Andrew Fletcher. Apart from the testimony of all of them, the most compelling reason of all is that again and again it strikes the authentic Fletcher note, conversational but passionate, lucid and bold, and determined to the last to uphold the independence of the Scottish Parliament.

These qualities in Fletcher earned him a remarkable degree of respect and admiration among his contemporaries, supporters and opponents alike. Few mention him without expressing this, often in language which is lyrical in its intensity. There is reference after reference to his unshakable integrity, a quality which was rare in that age, when a majority of the Scottish Parliament was about to yield to bribery and intimidation. George Lockhart of Carnwath, for example, agreed with Fletcher in his opposition to the Union, but as a Jacobite had little sympathy with his anti-monarchist feelings. Even so, his splendid *Memoirs and Commentaries Upon the Affairs of Scotland*

(1817 Edition, Vol. I, pp. 75-77) has the following description of Fletcher:

> "The thoughts of England's domineering over Scotland, was what his generous soul could not away with. The indignities and oppression Scotland lay under, gaul'd him to the heart; so that in his learned and elaborate discourses he exposed them with undaunted courage and pathetic eloquence. . . . (He) was so stedfast to what he thought right, that no hazard nor advantage, no not the universal empire, nor the gold of America, could tempt him to yield or desert it . . . He was a strict and nice observer of all the points of honour, and his word sacred; as brave as his sword. . . . To sum up all, he was a learned, gallant, honest, and every other way well accomplish'd gentleman; and if ever a man proposes to serve and merit well of his country, let him place his courage, zeal and constancy as a pattern before him, and think himself sufficiently applauded and rewarded, by obtaining the character of being like Andrew Fletcher of Salton."

At the opposite end of the political spectrum, John Macky was a Hanoverian agent who wrote notes on Scottish and English politicians for the Electress Sophia (Published in *Memoirs of the Secret Service of John Macky* in 1733). He uses very similar language to Lockhart: "Steady in his Principles, of nice Honour, with abundance of learning; true as the sword he wears and bold as a lion . . . would lose his life readily to serve his Country; and would not do a base Thing to save it." The Sir John Clerk of Penicuik of the day somewhat reluctantly yielded to the pressure of his patron, the Duke of Queensberry, and lent his support to the Union. He was therefore a political opponent of Fletcher; but a note of admiration, if grudging perhaps, comes through his comments in his *Memoirs*:

> "A man of Republican principles . . . a little untoward in his temper, and much inclined to Eloquence . . . not very dexterous in making extempore replies. He was, however, a very Honest Man, and meant well in everything he said and did, except in cases where his humoure, passion and prejudices were suffered to get the better of his reasone."

This virtually unanimous praise of Fletcher among his Scottish contemporaries was the more remarkable because, as they also acknowledged, he had some qualities which were more likely to win enemies than friends. As Clerk remarked, he had a quick temper. The strength of his convictions made him impatient of opposition. Some of his ideas, to use his own word, were "visionary". One can understand why Jonathan Swift, with his anti-Scottish animus, wrote in the margin of his copy of Macky's book, "a most arrogant, conceited Pedant in Politics; cannot indure the least contradiction in any of his Opinions or Paradoxes". Even George Lockhart saw these weaknesses; "In his private conversation affable to his friends (but could not endure to converse with those he thought enemies to their country), and free of all manner of vice. He had a penetrating, dear and lively apprehension, but so extreamly wedded to his own opinions, that there were few (and those too must be his beloved friends, and of whom he had a good opinion) he could endure to reason against him, and did for the most part so closely and unalterably adhere to what he advanc'd (which was frequently very singular) that he'd break with his party before he'd alter the least jot of his schemes and maxims." Fletcher's contemporaries evidently felt that this negative side of his character was of small account when measured against the strength of his solid qualities.

Fletcher's reputation soon became almost legendary. He was, wrote W. F. Mathison, "almost universally respected and esteemed". Sir John Dalrymple wrote of him as a man "whose mind was inflamed by love of the public good, all of whose ideas had a sublimity in them". David Hume described him as "a man of signal probity and fine genius". Sir Walter Scott expressed the general view when he said that Fletcher was "one of the most accomplished men and best patriots, whom Scotland has produced in any age". Fletcher became known quite simply as "the Patriot", an accolade which his countrymen have awarded to no one else.

The first sour note, apart from Jonathan Swift's marginalia, was struck by Macaulay. In his *History of England* (1914 Edition, Vol. II, p. 535) after praising Fletcher's "courage, disinterestedness and public spirit", he added this: "Yet he was no democrat. . . . It is a curious circumstance that this man, the most honest, fearless and uncompromising republican of his time, should have been the author of a plan for reducing a large part of the working classes of Scotland to slavery." In more recent times, Macaulay's lead has been followed by some other writers, anxious for their own political reasons to discredit

Fletcher. Even if it is a digression, it might be worth while to examine the basis for this attack. The fact is that Macaulay, great historian as he was, is guilty in this instance of insensitivity both to the material circumstances and the climate of opinion at the end of the 17th Century.

Macaulay's reference is to Fletcher's *Second Discourse concerning the Affairs of Scotland* (1698). (It is reprinted in David Daiches's *Fletcher of Saltoun, Selected Writings*.) In this, Fletcher addresses himself to the problem of the virtual famine then afflicting Scotland as a result of a succession of years of atrocious weather and poor harvests. Many thousands of people, as he says, were actually dying for want of bread. Others were driven by desperation to become beggars and vagabonds preying on the rest of the population. He proposes as a remedy for this that "every man of a certain estate" should be obliged to take a proportion of the "vagabonds" and put them to useful work, under strict legal safeguards. The employer would provide clothes, food, lodging to the worker and his family, and care for him in sickness and old age. He was, in effect, proposing a system of benevolent slavery, a desperate remedy to meet a desperate situation. The scheme had, of course, no chance of realisation, if only because the landowners, whose income also depended on the harvests, were in no position to accept such a burden.

Why then did Fletcher propose such a drastic scheme, exposing him to the charge of advocating slavery? He faced up to this in the *Discourse* itself. "Can any man, from whom such a thing has once escaped, ever offer to speak for liberty? But they must pardon me, if I tell them, that I regard not names, but things." It was possible, of course, that he was using a rhetorical device to awake the Scottish Parliament, to whom the pamphlet is addressed, to the enormity of the problem and to the responsibility of men of property to provide relief. It is written in a spirit of compassion: "And must not every unnecessary branch of our expense, or the least finery in our houses, clothes, or equipage, reproach us with our barbarity, so long as people born with natural endowments, perhaps not inferior to our own, and fellow citizens, perish for want of things absolutely necessary to life?" A few years later, in *A Modest Proposal* (1729) Jonathan Swift drew attention to the sufferings of the poor in Ireland by an ironic proposal that their children should be sold as meat. Fletcher's intention may have been equally ironic. In his own time, no one ever attacked Fletcher as a literal advocate of slavery, although he was in the centre of controversy for years. He devoted only one short pamphlet to the subject, unlike the central themes of his thought to which he returned repeatedly in his writings and speeches.

On the other hand, there was nothing new or unfamiliar in Fletcher's day to the idea that "vagabonds and sturdy beggars" should be compelled to work in a state of virtual servitude. Provision was in fact made for it in a whole series of Acts of the Scottish Parliament from 1579 to the end of the 17th Century, even if they remained ineffective except in coal-mining and salt-panning. There is a very full treatment of the whole subject in an essay in the *Edinburgh Review* (Vol. 189, January 1899, pp. 119-148) which describes it as "the favourite solution during the whole of the 17th Century of our still pressing problem of the unemployed". It was not a survival of mediaeval serfdom, which disappeared in Scotland earlier than in most countries, but a logical conclusion of the Calvinist work ethic. John Knox's *First Book of Discipline* said that "stout and sturdy beggars must be compelled to work". The work of Francis Hutcheson (1694-1747) was one of the foundations of the Scottish school of Philosophy and of the Enlightenment. He is described in the *Edinburgh Review* essay as "a most ardent and enlightened advocate of freedom", but in his *System of Moral Philosophy* (Vol. II, p. 201), he also proposed the "perpetual slavery" of "idle vagabonds".

The idea was then part of the accepted wisdom of the age as a desperate though ineffective response to the problem of unemployment and poverty, long before unemployment insurance and the welfare state were within the remote realms of possibility or imagination. Fletcher did, however, introduce some new elements into the discussion, the spirit of compassion the aspiration towards provision for education and care in sickness and old age, and the acceptance of responsibility by the wealthier part of the population. In a very real sense, as often with Fletcher's thought, it was an early and bold vision of the future. Ramsay MacDonald, in an article in the *Scottish Review* in July 1893 (Vol. XXII, No. XLIII) saw the point when he wrote: "No one who knows the scheme in its entirety, or who is aware of the conditions of labour in Scotland at the time, will regard the proposal as anything but humane—we might almost say enlightened."

Very few of the letters and private papers of Andrew Fletcher have survived. James Boswell when he visited Rousseau in 1764 persuaded him to write a life and undertook to provide information. (*Boswell on the Grand Tour: Germany and Switzerland*, (1953; p. 218).) Unfortunately, Rousseau did not complete the job and any papers that Boswell may have supplied have disappeared. There are, however, a few surviving letters which give us a glimpse of the private man. In April 1708, when he was imprisoned in Stirling Castle, he did not lose his spirit. He wrote to the Earl of Mar: "You may tell my Lord Calvin we are not locked up here at night; and that we drank all yesterday of the Collonel's good wine and continued till this morning, that we can find such company in Scotland" (Historical Manuscripts Commission: *Manuscripts of Mar and Kellie*, (1904; p. 436)). A few letters survived which Andrew Fletcher and other members of his family wrote during the last few months of his life. (Published in *Miscellany X* of the Scottish History Society, 1965.) They show that his compassion and concern for Scotland was alive to the end. In his last letter, written just before his death in September 1716, he sent instructions that "Two Hundred Pounds sterling value may be employed in relieving the most necessitous poor Scots prisoners or others who are rendered miserable by the late Rebellion". His cousin records that almost his audible words were: "Lord have mercy on my poor Country that is so barbarously oppressed."

The present short pamphlet does not, of course, display the full range of Fletcher's constitutional ideas. They find their fullest expression in his justly celebrated *An Account of a Conversation* (reprinted in David Daiches's *Selected Writings*). He saw national autonomy continued with international co-operation as extending not only to Scotland, England and Ireland but including the whole of a decentralised and balanced Europe. It is the pattern to which we are still gradually feeling our way nearly 300 years later. The history of Scotland would have been happier if Fletcher's constitutional ideas had prevailed in 1707.

P. H. SCOTT

Edinburgh, March 1982

Note

The text which follows reproduces the 1706 edition, including the spelling and punctuation. The only change is the substitution of the old letter 'f' by the modern 's'.

STATE

OF THE

CONTROVERSY

BETWIXT

United and Separate
PARLIAMENTS

Whether these Interests which are to be United by the present Treaty, and these Interests which by the same Treaty are to remain Separate and Distinct,

Are more properly and safely lodged under the Guardianship of an United Parliament, or under that of Separate Parliaments.

Printed in the Year 1706.

STATE OF THE CONTROVERSY BETWIXT UNITED AND SEPARATE PARLIAMENTS

Ever since the Union of the Two Crowns, it has been the work of factious turbulent Spirits, to foment Jealousies, and to promote Differences betwixt these Two Nations.

On the other hand, All well-meaning Men have thought, that a nearer Union will be the only effectual measure to bring these Two Nations to a peaceable State at home, and to make them formidable abroad.

Her Majesty in her Princely Care, hath been pleas'd to appoint Commissioners to treat of such an Union; and these Commissioners have concluded a Treaty for that purpose.

This Treaty is to be laid before the Parliaments of Both Nations; and no doubt this factious Race will still be at work, either intirely to obstruct this intended Union, or to put it upon such an uneasy and unequal foot, as shall tempt one or other of these Two Nations to break it.

The Consequences of a proper and well-founded Union, are so great and universal, that it may be the Privilege and Duty of every single Subject of either Nation, to offer his sincere Opinion in such a Case; and in the sense of this Duty I presume to offer these few Pages with all imaginable Sincerity and Submission.

I shall not pretend to make a particular Enquiry into the Detail of this Treaty; but this Scheme (so far as I can learn) and all other Treaties, whether upon the Incorporate or Fœderal Scheme, seem to conclude, That an absolute Communication of Trade, and of most other publick Interests and Privileges, with a proportionable Share of the Burthens and Benefits attending that Trade and these Privileges, is necessary towards establishing a just and lasting Union, and good Correspondence betwixt these Nations.

That Scheme likewise (and all other Schemes, whether Incorporate or Fœderal) seems to conclude, That in the most Absolute and Incorporate Union that can be made betwixt these Two Nations, there are several Interests (and of the greatest Consequence too) which are and must be reserved separate to each Nation, after the Union is agreed to.

It is none of my present purpose, to examine whether or not these Gentlemen, who were impowered to treat of this Matter, have acted their part faithfully and wisely, either with respect to the things to be Incorporated, or the things to be Reserved.

Whether the Duties which these Gentlemen have engag'd us in, are easy and proper for the Scots, as some say; or if they are insupportable, as others say?

Whether the Engagements which they have brought the Scots under, of paying a Share of the English Debts, will be sufficiently relieved by the Equivalents promised, or if the Scots will be over-whelmed by these Debts?

Whether the Rights of the Scots *Affrican*-Company, are well sold, or if they are thrown away?

Whether they have purposed good and substantial Articles and Provisions for the Security of our Scots Church, and Municipal Laws and Judicatures; or if they have slurr'd over these Matters, so as that the Treaty may be Risqued in Parliament?

Whether or not the Commons in *Scotland* are justly represented by 45, and the Peers by 16? And whether the State of Peers is honourably and justly treated; or if they are unpeered, debased, and degraded?

I shall shun all these Questions, and shall presume, that these Gentlemen have acted their part very faithfully in all these Matters, and have obtained very ample and substantial Articles and Stipulations, both with relation to the things to be incorporated, and the things to be reserved.

The great Question here to be consider'd, is touching the Security of these Matters; Whether the Performances of these Articles and Stipulations (such as they are) is more accessible and secure to the Scots after the Union, under the Guardianship and Administration of an Incorporated Parliament, compos'd of a small part of the Scots Members thrown into the whole Representative of *England*, or under the Administration of separate Parliaments? And whether or not an united Parliament will in its Consequences, engage and conciliate the Inclinations of the People of Both Nations for ever to maintain these Articles? Or if the Structure of an united Parliament will occasion such a Subversion of Rights and Families, as will be a handle in all Ages for shaking that Union?

Before I proceed to the Description of this Question, I shall beg leave to take notice of the Reception it had amongst the Commissioners of the Treaty in two Particulars: One Particular is, That this Question touching the united Parliament was the first material Point concluded on, though (with all due Submission) it ought to have been the last, for very obvious Reasons.

The Subject matter of this Treaty consists in two Branches; The things to be communicated or reserved of either side; and, The Government of these things after they are communicated and reserved.

The common Rules, both of Nature and Policy, do direct that the Things should be first adjusted which are to be governed, before the Government of them is pre-determined: There is no necessity of giving a Child its Name before it's brought forth: A Government to be made, ought to be adapted to the Nature of the things to be governed, and not the things to it.

If all manner of things of both Nations were to be incorporated, it was no doubt reasonable, that the whole parts of the Government of both Kingdoms should likewise have been incorporated with these things; but if otherwise, the Wisdom of the Treaters should have thought fit to reserve some things of Value, as a separate Property to each Nation: It would seem a reasonable Consequence, That a separate Property must be manag'd by a Government less or more separate, as the Nature and Value of that separate Property might require.

So that even though the whole Members might from the beginning have projected, that the whole Interests and Government were to be incorporated, yet in the common Rules of Business, the Articles of things ought to have been first adjusted.

The other Particular is, That when this grand Point came to be treated of, or rather pointed at, it was yielded without an Argument, though its known to every Body, that many of the greatest and wisest Men of this Nation are absolutely against an united Parliament, as a measure most likely to frustrate the Treaty.

I am very far from believing, that the reason for yielding this grand point in that manner can be justified, because (as is told) the English Treaters did positively declare they would not hear of any Treaty, excepting upon the foot of an incorporating Parliament: All the Treaters (as I have said) might have resolved upon it; but every thing must wait its time. This was not the way of treating with Men at Freedom, and with Commissioners called together by one and the same Authority. This was the only grand point of the whole Treaty; and the anticipating it thus, was yielding the whole Cause.

But I shall not insist any more upon the Journal of this Treaty; the Reasons of these preposterous Proceedings, and the Effects it will have towards the promoting or postponing of this long-wish'd for Union, will appear in due time.

I shall proceed to put the State of this Question in a true light, and shall use my weak Endeavours to undeceive some well-meaning Men, who seem to be amused with imaginary hopes of Security and Peace from an United Parliament.

I have taken notice that an Union does consist (with respect to its subject Matter) in two Branches, In things to be Incorporated or Reserved, and in the Administration and Government of these things, whether incorporated or reserved.

The first comprehends the People of both Nations, with their Trade, Privileges, Benefits, Burthens, and all other Interests.

An Union in these, is the only solid Expedient to unite and cement the Inclinations of different People, and therefore it ought to be as full and compleat as possible.

As for the Government and Administration of these things, it is only subservient to this Union of Interests, and it ought to be no further united as to its Powers, than in so far as it can be made answerable to its Ends.

Government may be distinguish'd with respect to its Power, into two Parts, The Executive and the Legislative.

The first is lodged properly in the hands of the Prince: The other has its rise from the People, with the Sanction of the Prince.

Government may be likewise distinguish'd, with respect to its Ends, in two Parts; One is for defending the united Property of the whole Subjects against Foreign Insults: The other is for protecting each particular Subject, or any Part or Number of the united Subjects, in the full and free Exercise of their several Properties, against mutual Injuries at home.

Each of these two several ends of Government, is accomplish'd according to the Will and Constitution of that Power whose Province it is.

And therefore as to the first end of Government, Nature seems to have pointed out a necessity that both these Nations should be govern'd by one Prince; their Situation is so contiguous, that one cannot be invaded but the other must be in danger; and if they were under different Princes, they might be in danger of invading each other: So that one Prince is the most proper Power for executing such Operations as are necessary for their common Defence.

But as to the other end of Government, an United Parliament is (with all Submission) a most improper Power to protect the Subjects in the several parts of this Island, in their united Properties, and far more in these which are to be reserved distinct and separate.

This will appear, by considering the Complexion of this Power of an United Parliament.

By the Constitution of Parliaments, the Laws are to have their rise from the Will and Humour of the People, signified by the Lords and Commons, who (in their different Capacities) are the Representatives of the Nation.

It is a certain Consequence of all Power, That whosoever is possess'd of it, he will imploy it to advance that Interest to which he himself is most affectionate, and in which he himself is most concern'd.

If the power of the making of Laws and Ordinances were in the sole Arbitriment of the Prince, no part of the Nation or Subjects would have any transcendent Influence in making Laws, more than any other part; the reason is plain, The Prince in that Case is Judge and not Party; he is no ways interested in these Laws, except in so far as they regard the common Benefit and Improvement of his whole Nation; he has no separate Property, no peculiar Neighbourhood, the remotest Corner is his, as well as the Metropolis; he finds his Honour and Government supported and secured by the Trade of the more remote parts, as well as by the Trade of the adjacent; and therefore he will encourage the Interest of the greater part, without suffering it to smother that of the lesser; he will not suffer any Branch of Trade in his whole Dominions, so perish by the Effects of Laws calculated for the personal Advantage of any number of his Subjects.

It must be quite otherwise, when Laws and Ordinances, relating to the Trade and other Concerns, are made by the Will and Humour of the People, there the Principles of Legislature flow from a quite different Fountain, and take their course into quite different Streams.

Amongst private Men, sometimes the Principles of Morality are the Rules of their Actings; but great Societies are above these Rules: A Member of Parliament considers himself as bound in Duty to maintain and promote the Interest he represents, by all the Latitude and Means allow'd in the Constitution; which in plain Language, is his Vote.

Seeing then every single Member of Parliament is both Judge and Party, it must necessarily follow, That if any Branch of Trade does Rival another, or if any separate Interest does contend with another, that Trade, and that Interest which has most Members to support it, must swallow up and diminish the other.

Having thus described the Nature and Complexion of this united Representative, I proceed to examine the Effects of its Power, with relation to the Interest of *Scotland*; and first with respect to these things which are to be incorporated.

In this long Tract of Land, from South to North, there is a great variety of Funds for Trade, such as Corn, Cattle, Fishing, Wool, Linnen, Coals, Salt, Lead, *&c.*

Among these many several Funds, there are some, which in their Use and Improvement are prejudical to each other, with respect to the Persons who are the Proprietors, and do naturally create a Rivalship in Trade; such as the Woollen in the South, and the Linnen in the North; the Importers of Cattle in the one part, and the Breeders in the other; the Pilchers in one part, and Herrings in the other; the Lace-workers in one, and the Clothiers in another.

It is very plain what Treatment the Scots may expect as to these Matters in an united Parliament; and if any Man doubts it, he may be fully satisfied, by examining the Deportment of the English towards one another, by several Acts past in their own Parliaments, such as these concerning Cattle, Flanders-Lace, Water-born Coal, *&c.* In which Cases, the prevailing Members of some Corners of *England*, have advanc'd their own Product and Manufacture by Laws, not only to the prejudice of another part which was not so numerous in Representatives, but even to the hurt of some of the most valuable Branches of the Product and Trade of *England*.

If the Subjects of *England* have been so treated by each other, how must it fare with the Scots, where the greater Extent of Territories by Land and Sea, (to omit other Considerations) shall produce a greater variety of Funds; some of which do more directly Rival the Funds of *England*, than those of *England* do one another.

For instance, Supposing an Act were offered in the united Parliament, for burying in Wollen all over the Nation, it would certainly carry by Votes, and the Scots Linnen would suffer by it.

Supposing the Pilcher-fishers in *Cornwall*, and the Red-herring Traders in the East and West Seas besouth *Yorkshire*, should find that the Scots Herring went to their Markets, and spoiled their Trade, it is plain, they can find means to clogg that Trade of Herring-fishing in *Scotland*.

In a word, The great distance of Ground from the South to the North, with the various and discrepant Funds of Trade, do naturally establish two distant Centers of Trade, to be carried on by two several Races of Men, who must have two distinct Views of Profit and Loss; and whatever Misfortunes the Scots have lain under hitherto, by the over-ruling Influence of their Neighbours, it is the finishing stroke to their sinking Trade, to abandon it by whole sale to the Mercy of that Parliament, which can now by out-voting the Scots, do that by Law which formerly was against the Laws of Nations, and did involve them in a state of Variance (if not of War) with the Scots.

But perhaps People may think these are but trifling Articles of Trade, and ought to give way to the other Blessings which they expect from this united Parliament, and hope that the 45 Scots Members may find favour with the contiguous English Members to join with them to support the equal Employment of these incorporated Interests; therefore I shall leave this point to the further Consideration of unprejudic'd Men, and shall proceed to describe the Fate of these valuable Interests which are expresly to be reserved, as a distinct National Property.

I shall pass over several Articles of lesser moments, which are said to be reserved in this Treaty, and shall only take notice of these four reserved Interests, as being of the highest Conse-quence to the Scots.

1. The separate establish'd Interest of Church-Government.
2. A separate State, or rather Species of Nobility.
3. Seperate Municipal Laws and Judicatures.
4. A separate Duty of an Equivalent to be paid by the English to the Scots, in recompence of that Share of the Debts of *England* which the Scots are to pay.

I shall demonstrate that as to the first and second of these, the English are under an indispensible Duty to demolish them; and that as to the third and fourth, it will be to the Interest and Advantage of the English to suppress them.

As to the first, it were intirely foreign to the present purpose, to enter into the debate in point of Right, which of these two Church-Governments is *Jure Divino*, or which of them is the more orderly, proper, or decent: What is necessary for the present purpose, is to take notice in point of fact, of these three several Principles; one or other of which does determine all Men in their Deportment towards Church-Government.

First, Most People are of opinion, that the Establishment of Church-Government is equally Sacred with that of Civil Government; that as God Almighty hath instituted one for the Preservation of the Civil Rights of Men, so he hath instituted the other for the Benefit of their Souls; and that his Vicegerent Powers, whether Princes, Parliaments, or other Assemblies, are each of them in their several Capacities, Executive or Legislative, bound in Duty to God, both to support and promote the Church-Governemnt which they think is right.

As a great many are of this opinion from a principle of Conscience, so a great many more are so from a Principle of Policy and good Government: These do think that the Government of Church and State are so naturally interwoven, that no Nation can be at peace, unless both these go hand in hand in their natural Duties to each other, and in their common Dispensations to the whole Members of the united Society.

A third sort of People (and not a few) are from a factious Principle, ready at all times to put Clergymen by the Ears, even where an Establishment by Law makes the one part secure, and a Toleration by Law makes the other part easy; and when two opposite Establishments shall appear in *Westminster*, and both shall pretend to claim their equal Rights in an united Parliament, these factious Men will never want a ready-handle.

Seeing then the Members of an united Parliament must be regulated by one or other of these Principles, it is very plain, that this united Parliament, must come to a Vote, Which of these Church Governments shall stand, and the other at best must satisfie it self with being tolerated.

Perhaps it may be objected against these Fears, that the ground of Contention will rather be removed, by two several Establishments of Church-Government, seeing the ground of Dissatisfaction was, because the one was not established as well as the other; that if two Churches are establish'd, both Parties will be satisfied, and those who are not pleas'd with the one, may go to the other: As to which, it shall be acknowledg'd, that the Subjects of both Nations may live easily under two different

Church Governments; and if these Two Nations were united in Trade, and other Interests, so as that the Subjects of Both should find equal Encouragement in either, it is not to be doubted, that both Nations might be more easie as to Church Matters than they are at present; but at the same time, these two different Establish'd Churches cannot be supported by one and the same Parliament.

And here appears plainly, the gross Mistake of those who imagine that one Parliament can support two different Church-Establishments; they do not advert to the difference betwixt being Tolerated and being Establish'd.

To be tolerated, is no more than to receive the Compassion of the Law, without the least share of Power, Incouragement, or Approbation.

To be establish'd, is to receive the Approbation, Judgment, and the whole Will of the Law; and a Church establish'd, is actually assumed into a share of the Constitution of the Government, with such a share of its Power as is proper to administer its own Discipline.

So that to say, one and the same Parliament will allow two Churches to be establish'd, each with separate Power, is equally ridiculous, as to say, that one Man can have two different Wills; and it is not to be doubted, that the first Act of an united Parliament, will be to reduce one of these incompatible Establishments; which of the two will fall, is easy to guess.

To illustrate this point, I shall suppose, that at the late Revolution, Episcopacy had been settled in the North, and Presbytery in the West (according to the Inclinations of these respective parts of *Scotland*) would not the World have lookt upon this as an incongruous piece of work; and would not both these Establishments have been jumbled into one long e'er now.

The Case will be the same, if the Parliaments of both Nations are as much united as that of *Scotland* is united in itself, with this variation only, that the Church-Governments of *England* and *Scotland* are more incompatible than Scots Episcopacy and Presbytery are.

Perhaps it may again be objected, that if these two Church-Governments are expresly secured by positive Articles, in this grand and solemn Treaty, no Parliament will attempt to alter them.

As to which, first, in point of fact, if this present Parliament of *Scotland* shall attempt to subvert the whole Fabrick of the Scots

Constitution, certainly *a fortiori*, an united Parliament may invert, or rather regulate a part of the Constitution; and therefore these who have any value for either the Church-Government of *Scotland*, or for any other of these reserved Interests, must of all things be careful to avoid so much as coming to a question, whether or not this present Parliament can finish this Treaty of Union; for if this Parliament shall so much as point at any such thing, there is an end for ever, of all the Security which the Scots can have for any of their reserved Interests.

But in the next place, in point of Right, it is plainly above the power of this Parliament to attempt any such Alteration in the Constitution; the reason is plain, Members of Parliament are but Administrators, and their Acts cannot extend beyond the Power given them by their Constituents; which is in general, to support or amend the Constitution, either by making new Laws, or by mending old ones.

And though Commissions to represent in Parliament, do run in general and most ample Terms, yet there is one natural Condition in all Commissions, which neither needs not ought to be express'd, *viz*. That the Undertakers of the Commissions shall contain themselves within the verge of the Constitution: If they exceed this, they usurpe a Power which is not given them; they violate the Constitution, and are punishable as Usurpers and Traitors.

After all, Supposing a new Parliament were called, and that the Members were fully instructed, and impowered by their Constituents to ratify a Treaty by which both Parliaments were to be turned into one, and that this last Scene of a dying Scots Parliament, and Scots Constitution, should take all the precaution which they could devise, for securing the present Establish'd Church-Government of *Scotland*, yet it is plainly beyond the power of Men, to make such a provision of Security as may not be undone in an united Parliament.

That Establishment, which was formerly safe under the Guardianship, Will and Approbation of its own Parliament, and of its own independent Constitution, is now turned out from under that shelter, and must take its Fate under a new sort of Parliament, and independent Constitution, where, if it has the Majority, it receives Approbation, and is assumed into a share of that new Constitution; but if otherwise, it may perhaps obtain Compassion and Tolleration.

It may be here alledged, That all those Dangers and Injuries by which the Scots suffer at the hands of the English, do arise from that State of Separation betwixt the Two Kingdoms, and that the more that this Separation is removed, the less the Danger will be; That an united Parliament makes us One and not Two, all British, and what is done in that Parliament is done for the British, and by the British.

As to which, I do so far agree with the Notion of an Incorporate Union; that both the Jealousies we are under, and the Injuries we receive, do arise from our present State of Separation; and therefore I am for uniting both Nations in all these Interests which are mentioned in this present Treaty, and some more, if so the Wisdom of the Nation shall think fit.

But seeing by the Scheme of this Treaty (and by all other Schemes that ever I heard of) there are some very valuable Interests to be reserved as separate Properties, and even as distinct Establishments; it seems beyond human Comprehension, how these separate distinct Interests, and Establishments, can be regulated and supported by one Parliament.

There are two Measures, which the Scots in prudence may take to skreen themselves from the unequal Power of the English; one is, To purchase their Affections; the other is, To avoid their Influence.

There is no honourable way for compassing the first, but by uniting with them, as I have said above; and if this will do the turn, where is the Necessity or Prudence of dismembring of a Scots Constitution, thorough so many Difficulties, Hardships, and Dangers: If this Union of Interests is not able to purchase entirely the Affections of the English, but that the English after such an Union in Interests, may still have an itching to out-rival the Scots in some of their united Interests, and shall still find themselves under a Necessity or Duty to suppress or demolish these Interests which are reserved to the Scots: In that Case, for the Scots to subject these Interests to an united Parliament, is so far from being an Expedient to avoid English Influence, that it is the way to throw themselves head-long into it; and the Scots deserve no pity, if they voluntarily surrender their united and separate Interests to the Mercy of an united Parliament, where the English shall have so vast a Majority.

The English can find access two several ways, to injure the Scots in their Trade, or other Concerns, By their Influence upon a Scots Parliament; and, By Law past in an English Parliament.

It is very plain, that they can practise the first of these means, with a great deal of more ease in an united Parliament, than in a separate Scots Parliament: It is much easier to corrupt 45 Scots at *London*, than it is to corrupt 300 at *Edinburgh*; and besides, there will be no occasion of corrupting them, when the Case shall occur, of a difference betwixt the South-Britons and the North-Britons; for the Northern will be out-voted, without being corrupted. As the first can be practis'd with ease, so the Scots may be injured in an united Parliament with greater safety.

A separate Parliament of *England* (especially if the Terms of Union are expresly declared) cannot make a Breach in the Interests of *Scotland*, without eminent danger to themselves; but in an united Parliament, they have the Concurrence of the Scots, even though the whole 45 should vote against the Law; and these 45 Scots Members do serve for no more than as so many Scots Witnesses, to assent to the surrender of such Rights as the English shall please to take from them, and to rise in Judgment against their own Nation, if they should afterwards pretend that any Injury has been done them.

In a word, a Separate English Parliament may perhaps invade the Scots Rights by their Laws; and perhaps a Scots Parliament may find means to move them to repeal those Laws: But in the case of an united Parliament, the Scots do make a formal Surrender of the very Faculty it self, and are for ever left to the Mercy of the English, with respect to all their Interests, both united and separate.

I shall close what I have to say, touching this Dream of being one and not two, by putting the Case, That a Law were offered in the united Parliament, (to make it go down the better) and that it were brought in by one of the 45 Scots Members, for some Regulation in the Church-Government, or for some Regulation of the Civil Judicatures, or touching some matters of Trade; and supposing, that whatever smooth Title this Law might have, yet it did point at no less than to over-turn the Church, or Civil Judicatures in *Scotland*, or to ruine the Trade of *Scotland*; I suppose the other Scots Members should oppose this Law, as being prejudicial to the Scots Rights reserved in the Articles of Treaty; The Answer is very ready and plain, That there is no such thing as Scots or English, they are all British, they are one, and not two; the Law now proposed cannot hurt the Scots no more than the English; if it does hurt, it does hurt to the British, of which the English are a part; and the only way to know whether it does hurt or good to the British, is to put it to the Vote of a British Parliament.

This will be the Issue of that darling Plea, of being one and not two; it will be turned upon the Scots with a Vengeance; and their 45 Scots Members may dance round to all Eternity, in this Trap of their own making.

I proceed to consider the next Scots Interest which is to be reserved, *viz.* A separate State, or rather Species of Nobility.

I am not here to examine into the Justice of that Proportion of 16, which I am told is by the Treaty appointed to be the Number for representing the whole Body of the Scots Nobility in the united Parliament, neither am I to take notice of the manner how they are to represent.

What I am here to observe, is, That by this Treaty the Scots, Peers are reduced into a new State; and upon this account, it may be very proper to consider, what Influence that new Species of Mungrel-Peerage may have upon the Union and Peace of these Nations, and what danger this new Sett of diminutive Peers may be in of being in time altogether supprest.

First then, That the Scots Peers are reduc'd to a new State, is plain; They have by the Patents of their Families, an inherent, proper, and constant Right of Sitting and Voting in Parliament; and by the present Treaty, that constant Right of theirs is turned into a meer precarious Right, either by Election, or by Rotation.

It is very obvious, what Influence the degrading of this State would have upon the Peace of these Nations: The Right of sitting constantly in Parliament, and of sharing in the Legislative Power of the Government, is as regularly the Property of every Peer of *Scotland*, as his own Estate is; and indeed it is more sacred and valuable, because the Condition of Man's Estate may fail, but that of his Representation cannot, without forfeiture.

The History of all Ages hath taught us, That single injured Families have been very uneasy to a Government; and that Government must be in a strange condition, which hath so great a number of Families in a state of Forfeiture; and these the greatest, and best allied Families in the Nation.

It is of no manner of weight, to pretend that their Rights are preserved by being represented by a small Number; and that besides, they acquire all the other Privileges of English Peers;

such as the Privilege of running in Debt without being bound to pay it, &c.

For first, If the Privilege of a constant Right is turned into that of Election, it is quite altering the property and nature of the Privilege: A Peer has in that case, less opportunity for sharing in the Government of his Nation, than a lesser Baron; and it is plain, that in process of time, an united Parliament would mumble this spurious Race of Scots Peers into nothing, for very obvious Reasons.

As to their acquiring of all the remaining Privileges of English Peers, these can never come to make near an Equivalent for that constant Right of Representation; and besides for a tast of their future Treatment in these matters, I am told, that even in the very Treaty it self, the Scots Peers are already justled out of one of the chief of these Privileges, *viz.* Their Right of sitting in Judgment upon the Trial of a Peer: But this is to descend into the Particulars of the Treaty, which I am to avoid.

I know, some Scotsmen do think that this State hath been encreas'd to a Number beyond measure; and therefore in retrenching the number of Peers, the Nation will not suffer.

I am very sensible, that this State is swelled (especially of late) to a very over-grown bulk; and perhaps there is too much ground to think, that some Men have been instrumental in encreasing the Number, of purpose to sink that noble Body of Men by its own weight, especially considering the mean and scandalous Grounds which some obscure People have most impudently offered of late, for their Pretensions to Titles of Honour.

Upon this account, the Nation may have an eye upon these who have been the chief Instruments in such Promotions; and it may become the Wisdom of the Nation, to fall upon Means to obstruct any such in time coming.

But as to these Gentlemen, who would run to that extream, of dismembring the State of Peers, I would recommend to their Consideration, the Fate of some Northern Nations, who enter'd upon the same Attempts.

Let no Man think, that it is an easie matter to alter any Branch of a Constitution: The fundamental Settlements of a Constitution are like so many Links of a Chain, when one Link is broke, the whole Chain is broke; and if one State of the Nation sets up a Rivalship with another, perhaps a third Party lies in wait to put the whole under Chains; and it is too much to be feared, that some People may have propagated these disorderly Notions with this very View.

Besides, These Gentlemen, who expect to ease the Scots Nation of a Burthen, by reducing the Number and Power of the Scots Nobility in this manner, will find themselves very wide of their purpose. If indeed a Proposal were made, for reforming that State, with relation to the Government, or Constitution of *Scotland*, as it now stands by it self, perhaps there might be some colour of ground to expect some Ease to the Nation by it; and even that must be attended with eminent Danger to the Constitution.

But if this Reform is calculated for the Case of the United Parliament, it is to take so much Power out of the hands of a Race of Scotsmen, who might some time or other stand in the Gap for that part of the Island where their Interests and Relations are, and to translate it into the hands of a Sett of Men, whose Biass lies another way, and whose little Finger may prove thicker than the others Loins.

I make not the least doubt, that there are some People in the Nation, who, from a prejudice at the present Church-Establishment, and the Nobility, would willingly sacrifice Both, hoping that they shall be able to secure their other Interests, which are of more value to them.

But these Gentlemen will find, that all their Interests will meet with the same Quarters; when an united Parliament shall take away one reserved Interest, this opens a Floodgate to sweep away the remainder.

I proceed therefore to examine the third Article of these Reserved Interests, *viz*. The Municipal Laws, and the Judicatures for administrating Justice, in which every individual Subject, of whatsomever Estate, Quality or Complexion, must be concerned to the highest degree.

I shall not be tenacious of the System of our Laws, though perhaps they are inferior to none; the Danger here pointed at, is, That the Judicatures for administrating Justice, and the Cognizance of all Law-Suits, shall be carried up to *London*, either in the first Instance, or by way of Appeal.

If this should be the Fate of our Judicatures, inevitable Ruin must follow: There is not any Man in the Nation, whose Affairs do not oblidge him frequently to attend the Session at *Edinburgh*; and even this is a very heavy Expence to those who live in the remote Shires; What insupportable addition of Expence will nsue, if in place of coming to *Edinburgh*, they must go to *London*, s not so much as to be thought of?

That this will be the Fate of our Judicatures, is too plain: It will begin with Appeals; and whatever Reservation we may pretend to make for a Scots Court of Appeals, the House of Peers will never suffer one part of the Nation to be from under their Jurisdiction, more than another; the Scots and English are no more two, but one, all are British; and it must be the Interest of a British House of Peers, to make all the British Subjects equally own the Jurisdiction of their House.

After Appeals, the Judicatures will soon follow: First they will lose their Authority, when People know where they can reverse a Sentence of the Session, they will not be very sollicitous what Sentence the Session gives.

Many Members of the united Parliament are Advocates and Attorneys at *London*, these will bring all the Scots Grist they can to their own Mill.

All the Representatives of these Towns and Counties which lie upon the Road, betwixt *Scotland* and *London*, will oblige themselves and their Constituents, by bringing so many Travellers into these places every Term.

In a word, it will even fare with the Scots, as it did with the Welsh, only with this Variation, that the more extraordinary Distance of *Scotland* from *London*, will make the Expense far more insupportable to the Scots than it is to the Welsh.

As these several Reasons which I have mentioned will occasion the Transportation of our Scots Judicatures to *London*, so I am told that there are some Clauses in the Treaty, which seem designed of purpose to pave the way for it, such as——subject nevertheless to such Regulations, as shall be thought necessary for the better Administration of Justice, to be made by the Parliament of *Great Britain*——That after the Union the Privy Council does continue in *Scotland*, for preserving of Order and publick Peace, until the Parliament of *Britian* shall think fit to alter it, or establish any other effectual Course for that end.——That all other Courts now in being in *Scotland*, do remain, but subject to such Alterations by the Parliament of *Britain*, as may be thought more expedient for the common Good.

I am to shun meddling with the Treaty, and therefore I shall make no Comment upon these Clauses.

Perhaps some People upon account of the personal Faults of

our Judges, may be willing to part with our Judicatures.

If there are any such personal Faults, let the Wisdom of a Scots Parliament provide a Remedy; to part with our Judicatures were a Cure worse than the Disease.

I come to the last of these reserved Interests, *viz.* a separate Duty of an Equivalent, to be paid by the English to the Scots, in Compensation of that share which the Scots are bound to pay o the Debts of *England*.

I am so much a Well-wisher to an Union and good Understanding betwixt these Nations, that I shall not insist upon the Value of our *Affrican* Company, which is to be abandoned for this Equivalent, and which many People think may become of more Value to *Scotland,* than all the Accession they can have by the Communication of Trade with *England*.

Neither shall I reckon up the vast Burden of Additiona Duties, which are to be laid on upon the Scots, which some People look upon as insupportable.

What I am here to observe is, that the Scots can have no manner of Security for this Equivalent, in the Case of an United Parliament.

In this matter of the Equivalent, the Scots do undertake to pay part of the English Debts, by laying on Duties upon their Customs, *&c.* And the English do undertake upon the other hand, to refund so much Money to the Scots, as an Equivalent This fixeth a formal Debit and Credit betwixt the Two Nations and it is not to be doubted that an United Parliament will bind the Scots to their part of the Performance; and they may look upon these Duties upon their Customs, *&c.* as unalterable; but it is very far above the Power of the Scots in that United Parliament, to force the English to pay their Equivalent.

It is incident to the depraved Nature of Man, that neither private Men, and far less Societies, will perform their Bargains or pay their Debts, unless where they are compelled to it.

In the Case of private Men or private Societies, the Judge at Common Law is Umpire; but in this Case of an United Parliament, which has no Superior Power to compel them, the English are both Judge and Party.

Whatever manner of way this Equivalent is to be disposed of it is certainly a Sum of Money to be paid by 513, and their Constituents, to 45 and their Constituents; and if any Man does believe that any 513 Men in the World, who have no Power to answer to, will compel themselves, and pay a great Sum o

Money either at once or yearly, he has more Faith than Experience or Judgment.

Thus I have laid open with all imaginable Sincerity, what I think must be the Fate of the Scots Interests (especially those which are to be reserved separate) in an United Parliament.

And this Scheme of an Union upon that foot, seems to be attended with many insuperable Difficulties.

All these Difficulties would evanish, if these Two Nations were united in their Interests under different Parliaments.

The English cannot apprehend the least Danger from the Scots in separate Parliaments, the only Ground of Discontent to the Scots is, because they are injured in their Trade and other Interests, either by English Laws, or by English Influence upon Scots Laws; If both are united in Trade and other Interests by express Articles, the Scots must be easy to the end of the World.

Neither are the Scots to apprehend Danger from separate Parliaments, as they may from an united One, for the Reasons I have given above.

Each separate Parliament will support their own Establish'd Church.

In the Case of separate Parliaments, there will be no subverted Constitutions and Privileges, nor forfeited Families, to rise up to disturb the Peace of the Society.

Each Parliament will maintain their own Civil Laws and Judicatures.

And each Parliament will manage their own Duties and Debts without imbroyling themselves with dangerous and uncertain Equivalents.

I know it will be objected, that to have different Parliaments, is to continue in the same unhappy State in which we have been ever since the Union of the Two Crowns.

This is a plain Mistake in fact, I do acknowledge that in Point of Right, the Scots by their Union in Allegiance were justly entitled to a Communication of Trade and other publick Privileges with the English, but the Misfortune lay in this, That at the Union of the Two Crowns, this mutual Right of Communication was not declared by some express open Deed; And the Scots (who are the weaker Nation) were left to plead their uncertain (though just) Titles before the Judicatures of *England.*

This Misfortune may be effectually provided for by an express Treaty, which will for ever secure the Scots in such

Articles as are to be expresly condescended to by the English
especially considering that the Errors of past times have been a
Warning to both Nations.

I know the Expense and some other bad Circumstances in the
Constitution of a Scots Parliament, is used by some as an
Argument for an United Parliament.

As to the Expense, a Scots Government may help that if they
please, but the Course proposed will not help it; the 45
Commoners, and the 16 Peers, with the Attendance of other
Scots Men at *London,* upon account of Parliamentary Business,
will be an Expense very far beyond the other, and will indeed
prove an insupportable Burden upon the Scots, especially
considering that in this Case the Money which is spent is all
carried out of the Kingdom.

As to the Errors in the Constitution of a Scots Parliament,
these may be helped by a Scots Parliament, if they who make
this Objection do not obstruct it.

But here again we meet with a frightful Objection, composed
of Despair and Fear, That the Scots can be no worse than they
are, and therefore they had best run into this Treaty at any rate;
That if they do not, theEnglish will never hear of a Treaty again,
and the Consequences will be Ruin and Desolation.

This seems to be a strange way of arguing, Shall the Scots
never find themselves in a Capacity of treating as Free-men?
Their Treaters have been hurried into this Article of an United
Parliament, and their Nation is to be bullied into it.

I appeal to every Man's own Observation, if (excepting a few
misled well-meaning Gentlemen) these Perswasives are not
handed about by those very Men, who have been most active in
drawing their own Nation into its present State of Misery;
These are the Incendiaries, who having fired the City, will not
advise or assist the Inhabitants to extinguish the Flame, but
would fright them away to save their Lives; And these are they
who have driven the Nation upon Precipices, thereby to force
them to swallow down such Terms as shall be offered them.

But it is to be hop'd, that the Wisdom of the Scots Nation will
take care equally to avoid these Precipices, and any such
dishonourable and ruinous Terms.

It is certainly the Interest of all good Men to promote a nearer
Union with our Neighbours of *England*; and no time ought to be
lost on our part in going about so good a Work; and the English
are no such People as these Incendiaries would represent them:

There are no doubt in both Nations, some People who endeavour to play the game of Faction to each others hand; but the wise and good People of both, have solid Grounds to go upon, for defeating these dark Projects, and for establishing a lasting Union and Settlement.

But if the English are not ripe for any such solid mean of Accomodation, the Scots as provident Men, are to consider, before they take such a Jump in the dark, whether or not they have any thing within the compass of their own Power, by which, without waiting for a Treaty with the English, they can make themselves easy and safe.

If we consider the Bounty of Providence to us in our own Native Situation and Product, and the Wisdom of our Ancestors, in leaving us a good wholesom Constitution; and shall compare these with our present degenerate State, we shall find a very large Field for improving the one, and for restoring the other, without the Concurrence of *England*.

I am not for over-loading the Power of the Prince with unusual Limitations, especially during the Administration of so gentle a Government as we live now under at present.

Neither shall I presume to prepossess the Deliberations of the insuing Session of Scots Parliament, by offering any thing that is new.

I shall only in a few general Terms, point out some things which arise naturally, as Expedients to obviate these Objections which are raised to drive this Nation into the measure of an United Parliament.

These Objections do point either at the Defects of our Constitution within our selves, or at the Defects of our relative State with respect to our Neighbours of *England*.

As to the Defects of our Constitution within our selves, I observe chiefly these Three Objections are made.

The Expense and bad Constitution of our Parliaments.

The exorbitant Number of our Nobility; and the Corruption of our Judicatures.

As to the Expense, and bad Constitution of our Parliaments, There have been some Laws lying before the Parliament for some Years, and some of them ready for the Royal Assent too; which may go a great length in curing of these Evils; and what more is requisite, may be worthy the Consideration of the ensuing Session.

As to the exorbitant Number of the Nobility, there is a Law

likewise lying under Consideration for some years, which may be a proper Remedy for obstructing their exorbitant Growth in time coming.

As to the Corruption of the Judicatures, the Lords of Session are secure against the Frowns of a Court, by having their Commissions *ad Vitam*: And seeing Corruption and Ignorance, are Failings very hurtful, but not easily to be proven; therefore, if the Parliament shall think fit, to pass a Law, for removing summarly by a Vote of Parliament, such Judges as the Majority of the Parliament shall think Corrupt or Ignorant; that Bench may become the best constitute Judicature in the World, and may be one of the most effectual means to make the Nation happy.

As to our relative State, with respect to our Neighbours of *England*, it is very plain, that in point of Right, the Scots by their Union in Allegiance with the English, are bound to share of the Burthens and Duties of *England*, and consequently are intitled to as great a share of their Trade, and other Privileges, as this Treaty does give them.

But lest some narrow selfish People should dispute this point of Right, I shall retire to an undeniable point of Fact, *viz.* That the Scots actually do contribute very largely and effectually to support these Wars, in which they have no other concern, but as being under the same Allegiance with *England*; and which are carried on for supporting that Trade, of which they are denied a share.

These Means, I say, of rectifying our own Constitution at home, are in our hands, in the Possession and Power of a Scots Parliament; and if the English doe not (without any further Treaty) make the Scots such suitable Returns, as both their just Rights and their ready Performances do intitle them to, it is both natural and just for the Scots to withdraw these Performances, and to turn them to the best Advantage any where else.

This they can easily do, either by publick Treaties, or private Bargains with some other Neighbours, by Acts of general or particular Naturalization, by declaring themselves a free Port, and by many other Measures, which are in the power of a Scots People or Parliament, without waiting for a Treaty with *England*.

It's true, in so far as an Act of Parliament is requisite, the Assent of the Crown must be had; but if a Scots Parliament does exert themselves according to their Duty, they have a Gracious Queen who will do them Justice.

As to Apprehensions of Opposition from the Power of *England*, it is in the power of *England* to do them Justice; and it is not to be imagined, that so wise and so generous a Nation, will endanger their own and their Neighbours Peace, where they can find so easy and so just a Remedy.

And besides, we see that the Justice of Providence hath inspired all the Potentates in *Europe*, with a Principle to preserve the Ballance of its Power; and new Alliances do arise every day, for protecting any one Part, tho never so small and contemptible, which is attack'd or injur'd by another.

In a word, If the Scots shall boldly, justly and dutifully, set about to rectify their own Constitution at home, and shall use their own Native Product of Men and Goods, to such Advantages as the Bounty of Providence lays before them, either by employing it with their Neighbours of *England*, who ought to have the first Offer of it, or by making honourable and beneficial Bargains elsewhere: The plain Consequence must be, either a comfortable State at home within themselves, or an honourable, equal, and lasting State of Union with their Neighbours of *England*.

FURTHER READING

There is no biography of Andrew Fletcher still in print, but two are widely available in the libraries. G. W. T. Omond's *Fletcher of Saltoun* in the Famous Scots series (Edinburgh and London, 1897) is brief but useful. W. C. Mackenzie's *Andrew Fletcher of Saltoun: His Life and Times* (Edinburgh, 1935) is the only comprehensive, full-length study.

Most of the known work of Fletcher is reprinted in Andrew Fletcher of Saltoun's *Selected Political Writings and Speeches*, edited by David Daiches (Scottish Academic Press, 1979). The events leading to the Treaty of Union, and Andrew Fletcher's part in the resistance to it, are described in P. H. Scott's *1707: The Union of Scotland and England* (W & R Chambers, 1979).